How to use this book

Follow the advice, in italics, given for teachers on each page.
Support the children as they read the text that is shaded in cream.
***Praise** the children at every step!*

Detailed guidance is provided in the Read Write Inc. Phonics Handbook

Children:

- *Practise reading the speed sounds.*
- *Read the green and red words for the story.*
- *Listen as you read the introduction.*
- *Discuss the vocabulary check with you.*
- *Read the story.*
- *Re-read the story and discuss the 'questions to talk about'.*
- *Re-read the story with fluency and expression.*
- *Practise reading the speed words.*

Speed sounds

Consonants *Say the pure sounds (do not add 'uh').*

f	l	m	n	r	s	v	z	sh	th	ng
	ll				ss		s			nk

b	c	d	g	h	j	p	qu	t	w	x	y	ch
	k							tt				
	ck											

Vowels *Say the sounds in and out of order.*

at	hen	in	on	up	day	see	high	blow	zoo

Each box contains one sound but sometimes more than one grapheme. Focus graphemes are ***circled****.*

Green words

Read in Fred Talk (sounds).

tap am elf sang mend red hat cash

box dress pink black doll big his

Read in syllables.

El`vis → Elvis

Read the root word first and then with the ending.

mend → mending thing → things

imp → imps doll → dolls

Red words

I you the my

Vocabulary check

Discuss the meaning (as used in the story) after the children have read the word.

	definition:
wand	*a magic stick used to cast spells*

Punctuation to note in this story:

Elvis	*Capital letter for names*
Tap His I Can	*Capital letters that start sentences*
.	*Full stop at the end of each sentence*
!	*Exclamation mark used to show anger and surprise*
...	Wait and see

Elvis

Introduction

Meet an elf called Elvis. Most elves mend shoes, but this elf will mend anything.

Even... let's find out.

Story written by Gill Munton
Illustrated by Tim Archbold

Elvis is an elf.
His job is mending things.

Tap! Tap! Tap!

"I am Elvis the elf!"
Elvis sang.

"I can mend
the witch's wand ...

Tap tap

I can mend
the imp's red hat ...

Stitch stitch

I can mend the king's big black cash box ...

Tap tap

I can mend the doll's pink dress ...

Stitch stitch

"Can you mend my socks?"

Questions to talk about

FIND IT QUESTIONS

✓ *Turn to the page*

✓ *Read the question to the children*

✓ *Find the answer*

Page 8-9: *What is Elvis' job?*

Page 10: *What does Elvis sing as he mends?*

Page 11-12: *List all the things Elvis has mended.*

Page 13: *Do you think he will mend the giant's socks? Why?*